Pikas

Victoria Blakemore

For Sandy, thank you for all of your guidance and support.

It's not about frogs this time!

Table of Contents

What Are Pikas?

Pikas are small mammals. They look like rodents, but they are actually closely related to rabbits and hares.

There are about thirty different kinds of pikas. They differ in size, color, and where they live.

Pikas are sometimes called rock

rabbits because they look similar

to rabbits and live in rocky areas.

Size

Pikas range in length from about five inches long to nearly nine inches long. Most are about seven inches long.

When fully grown, pikas weigh between three and ten ounces.

Male pikas are usually a bit

larger than female pikas.

Physical Characteristics

Pikas have large, round ears.
They help pikas to listen for
predators and for the calls of
other pikas.

Their paws are covered with
a thick fur. It helps to keep
them warm in the cold
weather of their habitat.

Pikas are a mixture of tan, brown, black, gray, and white. The color of their fur works as **camouflage** with the rocks of their habitat.

Habitat

Pikas are found in the mountains. They prefer rocky areas such as cliffs and the areas along the edge of forests.

It is often very cold where pikas live. Their thick fur helps to keep them warm.

Range

Pikas are found in parts of North America, Europe, and Asia.

In the United States, they are often seen in Oregon, Alaska, Washington, and Idaho.

Diet

Pikas are **herbivores**. They eat

only plants.

Their diet is made up of

grasses, flowers, and weeds.

Pikas often eat grasses during

the summer. They save the

flowers and other plants for

the winter.

Pikas use their sharp teeth to snip off parts of plants. They can carry a lot of plants in their mouth.

In the winter, it can be hard for pikas to find food. They solve this problem by storing food in their dens.

During the summer, pikas collect extra grasses and flowers. They lay them out in the sun to dry, then bring them into their den for the winter.

Pikas **forage** for extra food, then bring it back to their den in their mouth.

Communication

Pikas use mainly sound and scent to communicate with each other. They make sounds such as alarm calls and a longer call that is more like a song.

Pikas use their special scent to mark their **territory**. It tells other pikas that the area is taken.

Most of the time, calls are used

to warn other pikas. They chase

or fight pikas who get too close

to their territory.

Movement

Pikas are very **agile**. They are able to move quickly over their rocky habitat. They have been known to move as fast as fifteen miles per hour.

The rocks that pikas live among are uneven, so they often leap from rock to rock.

Pikas are good climbers. They

can climb up tall rocks and

rocky hills.

Young Pikas

Pikas usually have three babies in a **litter**, but they can have as many as five. When they are first born, they are blind and have thin fur.

Mothers take care of their babies for the first four weeks of their life. After that, young pikas can find food for themselves.

Pikas grow very quickly. They
are often fully grown by the
time they are three months old.

Pika Life

Pikas make a den among the rocks where they live. They each have their own den, but there may be many dens close together.

A group of pikas is called a colony. Colonies use special calls to warn each other about danger.

During the winter, pikas spend

most of their time in their den.

They do not **hibernate**, but they

are less active.

23

Staying Safe

Predators such as weasels, large birds, and foxes all hunt pikas. They have to be careful when they **forage** for food.

Before they leave the safety of the rocks, pikas look around for predators. They use a warning call to warn others if danger is near.

Pikas can hide among the
rocks, so they quickly run to
them if there is a predator near.

Population

American pikas are not **endangered**. Their populations have started to **decline** quickly, meaning that they could become **endangered** in the future.

The Ili pika, which is found in parts of China, is **endangered**. It could soon be **extinct**.

Pikas can live as long as seven

years in the wild, but they often

live about three years.

Pikas in Danger

The main threat that pikas are facing is rising temperatures. Pikas are **adapted** to living in cold **climates**, they cannot survive if it gets too hot.

When the temperature rises in their habitat, they have to move farther north. This can make it hard for them to find food.

Moving north can also make it hard for pikas to find enough **territory** to make their home.

Helping Pikas

Since most pikas are not **endangered**, they are not protected by any laws. This can make it hard for people to help keep them safe.

Researchers are studying pikas. They want to learn a lot about them so they can find more ways to help them.

Temperatures in pika habitats have been getting warmer. Many pikas have to move to colder areas where less food is available.

There are groups that are trying to help. They want to try to stop the change in temperature so that animals like pikas will be safe.

Glossary

Adapted: adjusted to live in a certain place or climate

Agile: able to move and turn quickly

Camouflage: using color to blend in to the surroundings

Climate: the usual weather in a place

Decline: get smaller, decrease

Endangered: at risk of becoming extinct

Extinct: when there are no more of an animal left in the wild

Forage: to search for food

Herbivore: an animal that eats only plants

Hibernate: when an animal sleeps during the winter to use less energy

Litter: a group of animals that are born at the same time

Territory: an area of land that an animal claims as its own

About the Author

Victoria Blakemore is a first grade

teacher in Southwest Florida with a

passion for reading.

You can visit her at

www.elementaryexplorers.com

Also in This Series

Gray Wolves — *Victoria Blakemore*
Sloths — *Victoria Blakemore*
Flamingos — *Victoria Blakemore*
Camels — *Victoria Blakemore*
Koalas — *Victoria Blakemore*
Honey Bees — *Victoria Blakemore*
Pandas — *Victoria Blakemore*

Pangolins — *Victoria Blakemore*
White-Tailed Deer — *Victoria Blakemore*
Orcas — *Victoria Blakemore*
Giraffes — *Victoria Blakemore*
Corn — *Victoria Blakemore*
Meerkats — *Victoria Blakemore*
Echidnas — *Victoria Blakemore*

Walruses — *Victoria Blakemore*
Raccoons — *Victoria Blakemore*
Bald Eagles — *Victoria Blakemore*
Apples — *Victoria Blakemore*
Arctic Foxes — *Victoria Blakemore*
Red Pandas — *Victoria Blakemore*
Cassowaries — *Victoria Blakemore*

Tigers — *Victoria Blakemore*
Ladybugs — *Victoria Blakemore*
Moose — *Victoria Blakemore*
Beluga Whales — *Victoria Blakemore*
Leopards — *Victoria Blakemore*
Elephants — *Victoria Blakemore*
Jellyfish — *Victoria Blakemore*

Binturongs — *Victoria Blakemore*
Lions — *Victoria Blakemore*
Dolphins — *Victoria Blakemore*
Reindeer — *Victoria Blakemore*
Hammerhead Sharks — *Victoria Blakemore*
Hippos — *Victoria Blakemore*
Pumpkins — *Victoria Blakemore*

Peafowl — *Victoria Blakemore*
Chameleons — *Victoria Blakemore*
Florida Panthers — *Victoria Blakemore*
Aye-Ayes — *Victoria Blakemore*
Black Bears — *Victoria Blakemore*
Cheetahs — *Victoria Blakemore*
Manatees — *Victoria Blakemore*

Gingerbread — *Victoria Blakemore*
Polar Bears — *Victoria Blakemore*
Hot Chocolate — *Victoria Blakemore*
Orangutans — *Victoria Blakemore*
Coyotes — *Victoria Blakemore*
Marshmallows — *Victoria Blakemore*
Strawberries — *Victoria Blakemore*

Also in This Series

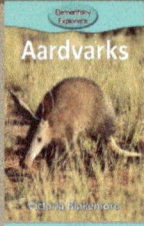

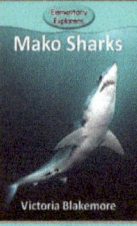

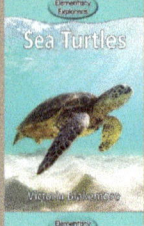

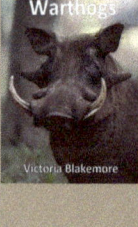

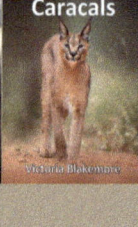

Aardvarks	Mako Sharks	Alligators	Frogs	Hedgehogs	Brown Bears	Bongos
Sea Turtles	Quokkas	Muskrats	Zebras	Red Foxes	Ring-Tailed Lemurs	Platypuses
Anteaters	Kangaroos	Rhinos	Jaguars	Wombats	Capybaras	Gorillas
Cats	Skunks	Butterflies	Dingoes	Snow Leopards	African Wild Dogs	Penguins
Whale Sharks	Wolverines	Warthogs	Caracals	Badgers	Seals	Hummingbirds
Pikas	Humpback Whales					

Victoria Blakemore

www.ingramcontent.com/pod-product-compliance
Lightning Source LLC
Chambersburg PA
CBHW051253020426

42333CB00025B/3184